D1237408

SAINT FRANCIS OF ASSISI

SAINT FRANCIS OF ASSISI

THE LITTLE POOR MAN

Fourth Edition

———————

From Water Colors of

P. Subercaseaux y Errazuriz, O.S.B.

Text by

Margaret R. Cullen

Published by
The Franciscan Missionaries of Mary
North Providence, R. I.

ST. FRANCIS AND HIS MOTHER

Donna Pica brought up her son in the fear of God. She also told him stories of knight-errantry which awakened in his boyish heart a great love for chivalrous adventure and heroic deeds.

CONTENTS

Foreword

Many are the books which have been written on St. Francis of Assisi. For more than seven centuries he has held the interest of multitudes of men and women, and the beauty and simplicity of his character still retain their own peculiar attraction for countless souls. In his day, in the thirteenth century, he was the apostle of peace and charity and perhaps, it is worth while even at the present, to bring out another edition of the unforgettable incidents related of him especially in the Fioretti or as it is known in English, *The Little Flowers of St. Francis.*

The accompanying illustrations have been made from the water-colors of Dom Pedro Subercaseaux y Errazuriz, O.S.B. and were painted by this distinguished artist in Assisi in close proximity to the convent of the Franciscan Missionaries of Mary.

He was born in Rome on December 10, 1880, and was the eldest son of Ramon Subercaseaux, the representative of Chile in France, Germany and Italy, and Ambassador to the Vatican for many years. His mother was Amalia Errazuriz de Subercaseaux, herself a gifted writer and one of the most charming and talented women of her generation in South America. Pedro was baptized in St. Peter's Basilica, hence his name. He showed very early that he had inherited the artistic spirit of the Subercaseaux, his father being well known in artistic circles as a brilliant connoisseur and painter. His artistic education started in the Royal Painting Academy of Berlin, was carried on in Rome and finished in Paris under the notable master Jules Lefebvre.

In March, 1907, he married Dona Elvira Lyon Otaegui, and after 13 years of happiness together they both agreed that they could make their lives more profitable to the Divine Master by dedicating them entirely to Him. With the consent of the Holy Father, Pope Benedict XV, they separated, she to enter the Congregation of the Catechist Ladies in Spain, and he, the Order of the Benedictines in the Quarr Abbey of the Isle of Wight.

In 1937, he was sent by his superiors in religion to establish the Order in Chile. In the beginning, he found temporary quarters in one of the beautiful farm houses some six miles from the capital. Now the monks are domiciled in their own abbey, planned and decorated by the founder. With a glorious background of mountains it is a thing of transcendent beauty and one of the notable show places for visitors to South America.

Amongst his other talents, Dom Pedro Subercaseaux is an excellent linguist, his English being more perfect than that of many an Englishman. Because of that, it was his duty and also his joy to show visitors around the historic Abbey.

Much of his best work has been done since entering the Order in the decoration of Churches and painting of religious subjects. In addition to these there are many examples of his art in important Government buildings on the old colonial life of South America and battle scenes of the war of Independence. His latest achievement is on the life of St. Benedict in fourteen beautiful water colors. Subercaseaux' most famous work is his series on St. Francis from which the illustrations in this book have been reproduced.

A younger brother, the Most Rev. John Subercaseaux Errazuriz, Bishop of Serena di Santiago, was killed in the summer of 1942 in an automobile accident.

All the pictures of Subercaseaux have been described as pictures of the man himself, in their fine conception, harmony of line, delicacy and beauty of color, and above all in their life. These qualities are especially evident in his work on the Saint of Assisi.

Like the illustrations, the subject matter of these stories is as old as the later years of the middle ages. At that period, *The Little Flowers of St. Francis,* were known to everyone in the neighborhood of Assisi. They may perhaps have an attraction for the twentieth century as well. The spirit of the Umbrian Saint is one of the precious things he left to a world which will never be over supplied with the sweetness and tenderness, the joy and gladness so characteristic of this chosen friar who lived the Gospel, loved poverty and preached to all the peace and charity of Christ.

MARGARET R. CULLEN
English Department
Cumberland High School

Approbation

In this little book, *Saint Francis of Assisi,* with its accompanying illustrations are to be found some of the features which have given him, across seven centuries, his supreme charm and attractiveness and have made God's little poor man, everybody's Saint.

There are many sweet incidents in the legends of the *Little Flowers* with a special appeal for boys and girls. To make them available for the present generation is a work well worth while and is the justification for one more book on the Saint of Umbria's vale.

As supplementary reading in classes in religion the work will have a real value. May it also find its way into many a home to introduce there the child of God who never grew old.

✝ Francis P. Keough,
Bishop of Providence

Introduction

By Johannes Joergensen

(Written for first edition of pictures)

No life of man, perhaps not even the life of Christ, was more subject to illustration than the life of the little Poor Man from Assisi. From the first rough picture on the coffin of the Saint down to the splendid and refined art of Maurice Denis in his masterly illustration on the *Little Flowers of St. Francis,* all the greatest names of art follow each other in uninterrupted procession. Herr Thode, in his voluminous book on the Beginning of Italian Painting, gives us the first of the series, and century after century is adding fresh names to the glories of Renaissance and Baroque art.

No wonder then that Franciscan inspiration is producing new works even in this century. The present lines are meant as an introduction (if such a one be necessary) to a new pictorial life of the Umbrian Saint. Pedro Subercaseaux — this is the name of the artist — is no child of Europe. He comes to us from over the ocean, and his cradle stood on the shore of another ocean, — yet farther away — he is a native of Chile. But there is European blood in his veins, and his spiritual youth took place on entirely old world ground. The Church of Rome gave him his intellectual and sentimental education, and Roman Catholic countries were the first goal of his wandering desires. The South American became a South European. The great shrines of Spain, the holy places of Italy, saw the young pilgrim from over the sea dropping his staff and kneeling down in prayer.

Kneeling down in prayer — and rising to work! The old maxim runs — Ora et labora — "pray and work." And Pedro Subercaseaux was no lazy idler, no sightseeing esthete, enjoying things of beauty only to himself. He was an artist, a poet, whose materials are not verse and rhyme, but line and color. His sketch-book was a volume of hymns on the beauty of Italy. Not that tourist-haunted Italy that goes from Bordighera to Sorrento and is only a continuation of the French Riviera, with or without Monte Carlo's demi-mondaines and suicides. But real Italy, true, rough, old-fashioned Italy — Italy of the small towns and the barren mountains, Franciscan Italy, to say all about it — Italy in the grey frock of the friar and the worn coat of the peasant. This Italy is the Italy of Pedro Subercaseaux. There he is at home and at ease. There he sought the Saint he loved — and there he found him.

Because this is the truth about the work of the South American painter — Saint Francis *lives* in it. This is no lifeless revocation of a story from the past. Turn the pages of the volume, and you will find yourself not only in full, real Italy, but also in full, real thirteenth century. You will remark (and how could you not?) the historical exactitude of these pictures. See for instance Francis represented as *rex festi,* king of the festival — the garments, the musical instruments, the vessels and cups on the table — all is as it really was in thirteenth century Umbria. Or look at the splendid historical reconstruction of the old basilica of St. Peter's with the *pigna* in the midst of the *paradiso*. But — well, another might do the same! I think Eugene Burnaud did — although with less detail. This is not the thing.

If you feel so great a difference between the cold, well-drawn pictures of the Swiss painter and the work of Subercaseaux, it is because the latter of the two artists *lived* it all by himself. He is in the same relation to the Umbrian Saint as for instance Boutet de Monvel was to *his* heroine, Jeanne d'Arc. Works such as those are not only expressions of art — they are expressions of life. They are not only speaking to the eyes — they are speaking to the soul.

And this is the reason why I appreciate so highly this new pictorial life of Saint Francis. Look at the young Assisi-merchant, praying down at San Damiano, before the old crucifix, and receiving the divine order "Go, Francis, build up My Church — you see, it is falling in ruin!" Follow him to all the places of passion (but of triumph too) which marked his short existence. See him — then at the end of his life, in the hut of branches and mud, listening to the angel, rapt in ecstasy — "And if the angel had sounded one note more, it should have been death!" — and you will understand with all your soul and all your heart, what a great thing Christianity is, and what a great Christian Saint Francis was. And this, I suppose, was just what Pedro Subercaseaux would have you understand.

JOHANNES JOERGENSEN

Assisi (Umbria)

A FEAST WITH HIS FRIENDS

Francis was rich and fond of spending money lavishly among his gay friends. The young noblemen of Assisi loved him for his merry and generous character, and Bernardone, his father, was proud to see his son in such fine company.

STORY I

Childhood of Saint Francis

Born in a stable, like our dear Lord
Was Francis Assisi, the herald of God.

Many, many years ago, in a little Italian town named Assisi was born a child who was to become famous. That infant was named Giovanni, or John, and as he was called *Il Francesco* (the little Frenchman) when he was young he is still known as Saint Francis of Assisi. There is an old tradition concerning his birth which says he was born in 1182 in a poor stable in the town of Assisi because his mother wished him to be born like our Lord. His father, a very wealthy cloth merchant, was called Pietro Bernardone; his mother, a member of a noble French family was named Madonna Pica.

There are many traditions still remembered by the people of Assisi about the birth of this sweet and tender Saint. A holy abbot was said to have foretold ten years before Francis was born that Umbria would produce a new order for the Church which would carry the light of the gospel everywhere. Another legend was that a strange man had come to Assisi and cried out in the streets, "Peace and Blessing will come with the little Bernardone." On the day of the Baptism of the child a venerable stranger had asked to be the godfather and another man unknown in the place had asked to carry him home from the church, kissed him, made the sign of the cross on his shoulders and told his parents to care for the child very faithfully, for he would do great things for God and man when he grew up. These little stories of the baby days of Francis show what the people thought of the holiness of the one whose name is always joined to the town where he came into the world.

His mother loved him and never spared herself in his training. Like everyone the Saint-to-be owed very much to his mother. He was her favorite and they used to spend long evenings together as the child learned his prayers and songs in French. He loved music so much that while still very young he became one of a group of troubadours or travelling singers and used to lead his companions though the hills of Umbria singing the songs of the day.

Not only was he the favorite of his family, but also of the townspeople. Handsome, gay, brave and courteous, he was the leader of every undertaking, liked fine clothes and loved pleasure. To have a good time was Francis' desire; the more money he spent, the happier he was.

When he was about fourteen he began to work with his

father and was given all the money he could ask for to spend on himself and his friends. His popularity made him a king of a "court of love" and his generosity made him a leader in parades and banquets which were held often in Assisi. And so Francis lived on having a good time, and disliking work until he was twenty years old.

"Father," he asked one day, "may I have a banquet?" Delighted, the father gave him a great amount of money. Francis prepared a glorious feast and dressed as a knight for the occasion. After the banquet, he led his friends through the streets of Assisi singing carols. Pietro and his wife gazed upon him with admiration. "Ah, perhaps now he will marry a rich girl and become a prince," sighed the father — "he will add glory to my name."

But Pietro was wrong. That was Francis' last feast.

Now, it happened that about the year 1205, war broke out between Assisi and Perugia. The soldiers of Assisi were badly defeated, and Francis with several other prisoners was held captive for over a year. During this time, he contracted a fever and waged a hard and bitter battle against death. Gradually, as he recovered his health, he began to realize what a useless, empty life he had been leading; he resolved to turn away from enjoyment and pleasure and in obedience to the voice of a vision to abandon a military career.

There is a great church in his native town in which his

life is painted on the walls. One of the pictures brings to mind a dream of the Saint. He saw, in his sleep, a grand palace filled with arms and a cross above them. "For whom is this palace and for whom are these arms?" he asked. A voice replied, "For thee and thy soldiers." Believing he was to be a soldier he marched off again to Spoleto to have a part in the war. Another vision came to him and he heard the voice a second time asking, "Who can do you more good, the Master or the servant?" "The Master," answered Francis. "Why then, have you abandoned the Master for the servant, the prince for the subject? Return to Assisi and there I will show you what you should do."

Soon after, Francis' mother secretly called him home. She was surprised to see her son so changed and knew right away that he no longer had any desire for fun and laughter and money; he no longer wanted parties and feasts; he no longer wanted his old companions. When they laughed at him, and jeered him, he remained silent.

One night when he refused to go with his associates, one of them said to him: "You're getting so absent-minded lately, you must be thinking of getting married." As he laughed, he answered: "Good guess! You're quite right! I am about to take a wife of surpassing fairness, the most beautiful around, and she is none other than Lady Poverty."

Now, remember that it must have been quite hard for

Francis to lead a life of poverty. Imagine your having everything you wanted – food, clothes, friends, money – don't you think it would be hard for you to give it up? Then, think how hard it was for Francis to give up his pleasures forever!

To show God that you love Him
And Blessed Francis too;
Just pray that Heaven's blessings
May be bestowed on you.

REMORSE OF CONSCIENCE

One day the young Francis dismissed a beggar from his father's shop. He was at once sorry for what he had done, and running after the poor man, gave him a rich present. From that day forth he resolved never to refuse anything that was asked of him in God's Name.

STORY II

Saint Francis and the Poor

For love of God, he gave up all
And answered Poverty's sweet call.

During his youth, Francis spent many days in idleness and pleasure. Dressed in velvet and brocade, he often rode his spirited horse through the streets of Assisi. He often dreamed that when he was old enough, he might travel to France to sell cloth to the knights and rich ladies of the court. That is why he was satisfied to spend some time attending to his father's business. He loved to measure cloth for the wealthy merchants who stopped to make purcheses in the little store. He was always happy to listen to their clever conversation because he thought he was making nice acquaintances. Being a proud and haughty lad, he attended only to the rich; he had no liking for the poor.

One day while managing the shop, he remarked that the poor people no longer came to buy cloth. He pretended to be glad, but deep in his heart, he continued to wonder why they ceased to patronize him. "Oh, well," he said, "I'll make lots of money selling cloth to the rich!"

Just as he finished, a figure approached the door. Old, feeble, and stooped, the man slowly and humbly asked for help.

"Help!" exclaimed Francis. "Get away from here, for I have nothing for you — go elsewhere to do your begging."

"Very well," replied the poor, weak beggar. "I'll beg your pardon and leave, but first I'll pray that God may soften your hard heart."

As he left the doorway, he could not hold back the tears. He wondered how he could continue on his way. No food, no money, just rags for clothes, and yet he could receive no help. However, he did not give up. "God will take care of me" was his constant thought.

Francis, on the other hand, was not so easily pacified. Looking at the pitiful figure in ragged clothing trudging down the street, he became repentant. Forgetting the customers for a moment, he said aloud, "Whatsoever you do to the least of mine, you do unto Me — Give a drink of water in My name" — all he wanted was a drink of water and I refused it just because he wasn't a lord or a noble or a duke. No, he wasn't a king, but truly was a messenger from the King of kings.

Immediately he left the shop, ran down the street and overtook the beggar. With a sincere apology, Francis asked the poor old man to accept a large sum of money which was pressed into his trembling hand.

Then and there, Francis decided to give his life for the poor. Taking all his worldly possessions, he left his father's store and started out to aid them. First, he turned his attention to the poorest people of Assisi. By this time he had forgotten all selfishness, as he considered the happiness that his help could bring to poverty-stricken children. He traveled along on foot until darkness fell, passing money to all beggars along the way. His last penny was gone and he had no place to spend the night. Tired and weary from walking for several hours, he looked around for a sheltered spot; finally, he spied a large stable in the distance. Satisfied that he had found a refuge, he thanked God and secretly thought, "My Lord must be showing me a special favor when He finds for me the same kind of shelter that He had on the first Christmas night."

The next morning, he again journeyed on, asking God to put a beggar in his path. He had not far to go, before meeting a half naked mendicant outside a church door.

Francis instantly said, "Now, here's my chance to know what real poverty is like." So, he changed his velvets and brocades for the rags of the beggar and stood outside the Church door for the whole day asking alms for God's poor.

That night he slept in the cellar of the Church.

Some days later, on the verge of starvation he went to Christ, the good priests fed him and welcomed him into their the Chapel of St. Damien and asked for food. In the spirit of home for many days. Suddenly, one day Francis told them not to bother further, as he was to leave at once.

Just as twilight was falling, he decided to procure an evening meal for himself. Going from door to door through the town of Assisi he obtained scraps of food which the housewives could not use. This repast, I am sure, would not be very savoury to your taste, but the little band of beggars sat on the steps of an abandoned building and liked it just as much as Francis had enjoyed the delicious meals of his youth.

What a transformation in a young man! The richest lad of Assisi now a poor tramp in the streets; he had no home, gave away all the money that he collected, so that he was always penniless, had very little food, and his clothing was little more than an old robe, tied around the waist with a rope. And, in spite of all this, he was happy! So happy, in fact, many people followed his example, wandering about the countryside, rendering aid to the helpless. Francis called this little band his "Brothers" or "Friars" – twelve in number like the Apostles of Our Lord.

As time went on, they were able to establish a home for themselves – a place where beggars were welcome day and night. Their way of living was no different from that of the poor people of the street. Very often, they gave up their meals so that some one else might not be hungry; many times they gave up their beds, so that another one, less fortunate than they, might not sleep on the floor.

As Christmas was drawing near, the "brothers" decided to surprise Francis and have a better meal than usual. The room in which the table was set, was gaily decorated with holly and laurel.

Dinner time approached and the "friars" summoned Francis to the table; in utter dismay he looked at the feast spread upon the table, displeased because his followers had been extravagant while others were starving, he took a small piece of bread and ate it as he sat on the floor at the corner of the table. In tears, the "brothers" begged his pardon and profited by his lesson of true poverty and humility.

It was very hard for Francis to carry on his work because he always hesitated to accept money; he would rather take food, clothing and other necessities, for he thought that in gathering money, he was not really poor.

He knew that his mother was very unhappy watching him walk the streets of Assisi in his bare feet. He realized that his father could not forgive him for selling the cloth and the horse. Hardest of all, he was aware that people, his family and friends, scorned him and tried to make others hate him.

Page Thirty-one

But, in spite of all this, he carried on, because he knew that his torture could never be so severe as the agony of Christ on Calvary.

The angels of Heaven beamed down on him
As he went from day to day
Loving and helping and feeding the poor,
Trying to brighten their way!

MEETING A LEPER

One day Francis met a leper, and his first impulse was naturally to avoid the poor creature. But reflecting that God wished him to love those whom he had hitherto despised, he dismounted from his horse and not only gave the leper money but embraced him tenderly. He returned home full of unutterable joy at having thus conquered his feelings.

STORY III

Saint Francis in His Youth

Two wandering souls in Umbria
While on their journeys meet
The Saint stoops to the leper
The bitter becomes sweet.

Towards the end of his days, St. Francis composed what is known as his Testament. He gives the first place in it to his experience with a leper. He met this poor man on a plain in Umbria. He remembered and repeated what occurred, just as almost anyone might carry in his memory across his life something strange or unusual that happened when he was young.

"The Lord gave me the grace," he wrote, "to begin thus to do penance. While I was still in sin it seemed to me too hard a thing to see lepers; but the Lord Himself brought me into the midst of them and I practiced mercy toward them. When I retired from their presence, that which had seemed so bitter was changed for me into sweetness for soul and body. After which I delayed little and quitted the world."

It is possible that this meeting with one of God's invalids, as lepers were called in the Middle Ages, brought to Francis a beginning of the many later graces which made him a Saint. The leper who rose in front of him to ask for help as he was riding along was the inspiration by the grace of God for a sublime work of charity. With the help of God, Francis overcame the feeling of disgust that arose in him. He sprang to the ground, gave aid to the afflicted one and kissed his hand.

Getting back on his horse, he looked around for the sufferer, but the plain was deserted. There was no one to be seen. This kindness of Francis drew toward him many souls, anxious to show their love for God, and he created in them a real spirit of charity for the poor lepers.

One grace followed another after this. The thought came into his head that he should go to Rome. He lived in the days when many people made pilgrimages to see the Pope. After the long journey Francis stood in the square before St. Peter's, the greatest church in the world. He entered to look at the tomb of the Apostle and emptied his pockets of all that he possessed in the place where the first Pope was venerated. Going outside he exchanged clothes for those of a poor beggar and for the rest of the day remained there fasting and begging.

Soon after his return from the Holy City to Assisi, he

found himself one day in the Church of St. Damien. Kneeling there before an ancient crucifix, he prayed as did St. Paul, "O Lord, what would you have me do?" He received an answer as soon as his prayer was over. "Go and build My Church which you see is in ruins," came to him from the lips of the figure on the cross. So he went to his father's shop and bundled together a load of drapery cloth; then he mounted his horse, went to the business section of Foligno and sold both horse and cloth to obtain money to repair the church. When the priest found out how Francis had obtained the money, he refused to accept it. He then asked that it should be used to keep a lamp burning before the crucifix; this also was refused. Francis then threw it through a window of the church as it was of no use to him. The pastor received him into his house and kept him there until his father descended one day to St. Damien's.

Pietro was enraged. Bad enough for his son to be a coward — but now a thief! He could not control his anger. He demanded that the money be refunded. If Francis did not comply with his wishes at once, he would take him to court.

In fright, Francis went to a cave near St. Damien's and hid there for a month. When, finally, he left his hiding place, dirty and starved, a great crowd gathered, following him through the street, hooting, mocking and pelting him with stones and mud. Then, he was dragged home by his father, beaten with a whip, bound with ropes, and locked in a dark closet.

As soon as Pietro left the house, Francis' mother freed him. He returned to St. Damien's at once to seek shelter from the priests. His father was not satisfied with the punishment; he decided now to disinherit his son.

"How happy that makes me!" exclaimed Francis, and returning all his belongings, even his clothes, to Pietro, he added: "Until now I have called you my father on earth; from now on I shall say only, 'Our Father, who art in Heaven'!"

Francis then wandered off into the hills behind Assisi singing hymns of praise along the way. As he walked along slowly and peacefully, he was stopped by two robbers.

"Who are you?" they asked scornfully.

"I am the herald of the great King," he answered. In a flash, they attacked him, and threw him into a snow drift, hoping he would freeze to death. But Francis was not to be subdued. He crawled to a neighboring monastery where he worked for a time as a cook. Some time later, he left there for Gubbio where he borrowed a cloak. His next step was to return to the church of Saint Damien. He could not forget what he had heard from the voice that had come to him there. Within the hour he was again in the town of Assisi where he gathered up a few stones and with great labor carried them back to St. Damien's. Having erected a rude scaffolding he used it as a pulpit to exhort the passers-by to come to his assistance. "He who gives me a stone," he said, "shall have a reward; he who gives me two stones shall have two rewards; and he who gives me three, as many rewards."

After he had completed the work on St. Damien's he went to two other churches. Many of those who helped him from the time when he began this task followed him to the next places, and soon three buildings had been repaired. Francis began to think that the words, "Go build up My church," might have a wider meaning than the placing of stones where they should be. He felt that his vocation to build up the church among the people was the will of God and the real meaning of the message from the crucifix. His future became clearer as the days went on and it was not long before he was busy building up the Church in the souls of all to whom he could teach his gospel of peace and charity.

Many great men of the thirteenth cenury looked upon Francis with respect and admiration for his great zeal; in fact, they were so impressed, that they decided to join with him to have a share in such wonderful work — and, thus, started the great Franciscan Order, whose members today go to far away countries to do just what Francis did; namely, to build Christ's Church.

It must have been discouraging for Francis to continue under many heart-breaking difficulties; but notice that he didn't falter; he was brave, just as you must be. God will help you in many ways if you make yourself like St. Francis and say often.

Jesus dear, I've done my best
I've tried in every way
To help Your friends for love of You,
Oh! bless my work, I pray.

THE CHRISTMAS CRIB

On Christmas night the clergy and people of Greccio were invited by Saint Francis to keep Christ's Nativity with him. An ox, an ass, and a manger with straw had been brought into a rustic cave where solemn Mass was sung. Then Francis spoke devoutly to the people about the birth of Jesus, after which some saw a little child asleep in the manger who woke up when the saint took him in his arms.

STORY IV

How Saint Francis Made the Crib

Like Bethlehem's stable long ago,
Where Shepherds once adored,
The hillside crib became that night
A temple for our Lord.

When Christmas comes, a figure of our Lord as an Infant is placed in a crib in the church. It is the same as the shepherds saw in Bethlehem. Look in and you will see a babe "wrapped in swaddling clothes and lying in a manger."

Now, the crib in our church is very much like the one the shepherds saw. It has a statue of a little baby. He is lying on the straw. Standing nearby there are two statues of a man and woman. They are Mary and Joseph. There are many shepherds kneeling on the straw, adoring the Christ Child. An ox, an ass and some sheep are standing nearby. The manger is covered with real evergreen trees. The little lantern hanging from the top is like the one in the first manger. Everything about the crib looks very poor and simple, because the manger in which Jesus was born was only a stable in a cave in Bethlehem.

That crib was not very beautiful; that is, it was not beautiful until Jesus came into it, and then, of course, it was the most beautiful place in the whole world.

This is the story of the crib of Bethlehem.

Mary, a beautiful Jewish maiden, and Joseph, a carpenter of Nazareth, were walking along the ways of Judea to Bethlehem. It was getting dark and they were trying to find a place to stay for the night. They knocked at the door of a small house. The answer was, "No room." They knocked at the door of the next, a bigger house, and the answer was, "No room." Again and again, they tried, but had no success. Joseph decided they could find shelter in the inn. But they received only the same cold, harsh answer.

How would you feel to be on a lonesome street at night when it is very dark, and have no place to stay? Imagine how sad Mary and Joseph were when no one would take them into their house.

Well, they walked until finally they found a cave — a stable — in which there were only an ox and an ass and a manger. It was very dark and very cold. There were no electric lights as you have today — only a lantern which Joseph carried; there was no stove to keep them warm. Now, it was in this cave that Jesus Christ was born at midnight. Joseph and Mary made a crib in the manger; they had no blankets to put on Jesus to keep Him warm; the only quilting that He had on His crib was straw.

Now, at this same time, there were shepherds watching their flocks in the nearby hills. Suddenly, a beautiful angel from Heaven came to them. Of course, they were afraid, because they had never seen an angel before. "Fear not," he said, "for I bring you tidings of great joy, for this day there is born to you a Saviour who is Christ, the Lord." As the angel spoke, a great crowd of angels appeared, saying:

"Glory to God in the highest; and on earth peace to men of good will."

The shepherds decided to go to Bethlehem; there they found Mary and Joseph and the Babe. They fell to their knees adoring the Infant Jesus. They looked upon Jesus, Mary and Saint Joseph who changed a lowly cave into a wonderful temple. People came from far and near to look at and to worship Christ. A star guided some, such as the Magi; heavenly music guided others; the message of the angels brought still more. Some of these brought rich and costly gifts to the Child, but none was so precious to Him as their love.

Now, all this happened almost two thousand years ago, and in all the years that have followed there have been millions and millions of men and women and little children who loved Jesus. They all wanted to do something to prove

BEFORE POPE INNOCENT III

At Rome Pope Innocent III, having heard of the Brothers through Cardinal John of Saint Paul, received them with kindness. He sanctioned their way of life, bade them preach penance wherever they went, and promised further approbation for the order when their numbers should have increased.

to Him just how much they loved Him; they knew that no matter how much they did for Him, He always did more for them.

Francis, too, wanted to tell about Jesus' birth; Christmas was a favorite feast. He would show the people a real Bethlehem Crib. In the year of Our Lord, 1223, Francis was living in a little town in Italy called Greccio. That little town, I think, was probably like Bethlehem — with its little streets, and beautiful hillsides — its sheep grazing in the pastures, its horses and donkeys walking in the roads.

Francis was so happy about his thought of having a real crib that he went to the Pope to seek his permission to carry out this wonderful idea. Pope Honorius immediately consented and Francis began at once. First, he called upon a friend, John Velita, to help him.

"Nothing could make me happier!" exclaimed John. "But we have but two weeks to Christmas, so we must hurry. I'll set out immediately to see if I can find a cave resembling that of Bethlehem."

He thought of a tree-covered hillside. There was a rocky cavern at the foot.

"That will be just the thing," said John.

He and Francis built stalls and filled the manger with straw. In it, they placed a statue of the Infant Jesus. They scattered straw on the floor and put statues of Mary and

Joseph on either side. Then, to make it just like Bethlehem they brought animals in from their pastures and placed them near the crib. As Francis and John were leading an ox and an ass to the stable, they saw sheep grazing on the hillside; the flock made the Saint and his companion think of the first Christmas in Bethlehem, so they completed the crib with several sheep.

Francis then thought of the celebration of Mass there at midnight on Christmas Eve. How happy all the people in the village would be, if they could see the real picture of the scene in Bethlehem! John helped Francis to gather evergreens to put in back of the manger. The dark green of the trees made a beautiful sight, mingled with the bright colors of flowers and the lighted candles on the altar.

Christmas Eve arrived. The bells of the town rang out that it was midnight. The whole earth was very dark and still, as the entire village of Greccio flocked to the cave to hear the Midnight Mass. Everybody sang the *Gloria in Excelsis*. After Mass Francis went to the Crib and took the statue of the Child in his arms. As he did so, the Child awoke and there was a little circle of golden light around His head. All the people were so surprised at this sight that they fell to their knees and adored the Infant just as the shepherds had done hundreds of years before.

Francis and the Order of Franciscans, which he founded have always made Christmas beautiful for everyone, even those in deserts, jungles and the many lands far away from here, where little children don't know much about Jesus, Mary and Joseph.

The crib in our churches resembles the one in Bethlehem, and the one made by St. Francis. It shows us how poor the birthplace of Jesus was, and it shows us also that He is there for us. As Christmas day dawns, we go to the Christ-Child's crib; give Him our hearts so full of love and say:

Dear Infant Jesus in the Crib
I come to tell my love,
To thank You for Your graces
And ask blessings from above!

SAINT CLARE'S INVITATION

Francis preached in the Cathedral of Assisi. Among his hearers Lady Clare, the daughter of Count Scifi, was inspired to offer herself wholly to God, and sought the saint's advice. Francis was glad to have won such a beautiful soul for the glory of his Master, and it was arranged that Clare should secretly leave her home and receive the religious habit.

Vocation of Saint Clare

God's chosen creature, Sister Clare
Abandoned wealth for alms and prayer.

While Francis was going about the countryside of Italy preaching, he did not realize that among his listeners was one more ardent than the rest; he did not know that there was in his gatherings a young maiden who longed to help him in his work. In fact, her interest was so great that she began to devise plans whereby she too might dedicate her life to God.

Her name was Clara Scifi, and she lived in Assisi where everyone admired and respected her because of her piety. Donna Ortolana, her mother, was a noble; she was indeed very proud of her beautiful daughter. As she gazed upon Clara's golden brown curls and sparkling blue eyes, she would say "All earth's beauty centered 'round a heavenly soul."

Now, Donna Ortolana had two other daughters of whom she was equally proud — Agnes and Beatrice, both younger than Clara. Their life was very happy as they played and worked together; it was truly much more joyous than that of the youngsters who were forced to go like soldiers of an army on the Children's Crusade.

This was a long time ago, in 1212, when an army of 30,000 children, all under twelve years of age, was formed under the leadership of Stephen, a French shepherd. He declared that God had called him to help to rescue the Holy Land from the Mohammedans. The Christians of Europe said that it was unfitting that the place where Christ lived and died, should be owned by His enemies. And so, taking the Cross as their insignia, they waged the famous wars, now known as the Crusades.

The children started out with the hope that when they reached Marseilles, the waters of the sea would divide, so that they could get across to Palestine. Bitterly disappointed because the water didn't move, many of them went home, but several thousands were kidnaped by merchants on seven ships. Two of the vessels were wrecked and all the other children were sold in slavery.

Clara and her sisters were fortunate in avoiding that terrible war. While all those horrible events were taking place, the Scifi children were enjoying themselves in their beautiful garden in Assisi.

One bright day in the Spring when she and her sisters had ceased playing, they went to sit at the edge of a brook to look at their shadow in the water. The sun was shining on the tiny waves as they rippled in the breeze and the girls were thinking and pondering over many things. Finally Clara said, "You know, my sisters, the ripples pass along the brook, suddenly disappear, and we never see them again. Well, just now I was thinking that I must be like that brook. Every day slips by, and the next brings nothing new to me. I wish I could go to the Holy Land to be a Crusader, and, perhaps, I could be a martyr. Don't you think it would be wonderful to be a martyr and go to Heaven to be with God forever and ever?"

She stopped suddenly, for a figure had appeared beside her. Her mother! How angry she was! Her one desire for her daughter was that she would marry the famous Count Merci.

"Go to your room now," ordered her mother, "and put on your very finest gown because Count Merci is coming this evening."

Clara was downhearted, but she knew that she must obey. Her dissatisfied smile did not escape the eyes of her parent, who added:

"Remember, dear, he is wealthy and his name bears great prestige and glory; you should be happy that he has chosen you to become his wife."

Time passed and Clara became more discontented.

Page Sixty-one

RECEPTION OF SAINT CLARE

On the evening of Palm Sunday Lady Clare, in the company of an aunt, came to Saint Mary of the Angels where Francis and his Brothers were awaiting her. He cut off her hair, gave her a grey habit, and took her to a convent of nuns where she stayed for some time. Later she settled at San Damiano with several other Sisters.

However, a memorable day of her life soon dawned. One Sunday morning, her mother and father had invited Count Merci to attend Mass with them at San Georgio to hear a Lenten sermon. After the celebrant had read the Gospel, he turned to the congregation and announced that the sermon would be preached by a young man who had received the Pope's blessing. His name was Francis.

His simple, forceful words so overwhelmed Clara, that she decided right then and there to make known her rejection of Count Merci, and to announce to her parents that she intended to become a follower of Francis.

After Mass, she told her story to Francis from whom she obtained the encouragement and advice she needed.

The days of Lent were swiftly passing, for Palm Sunday was at hand. The choir of San Georgio sang beautiful hymns of God's victory, as the priest distributed palm branches. Clara prayed and made her plans. She would leave for the Portiuncula Chapel as soon as possible.

Her preparations were completed and on Monday of Holy Week, in darkest night, she stole out of the house, accompanied by two companions. When they arrived at the monastery, they were received by Francis and his friars who marched in procession carrying lighted torches — the symbol of their faith. The ceremony of profession was then performed. Clara became a nun of Christ! She could now carry on Francis' work for Almighty God.

She listened carefully as Francis read, "For what doth it profit a man if he gain the whole world and suffer the loss of his soul?"

As she took her vows of poverty, chastity and obedience she thought, "Besides Thee, O Lord, what do I desire on earth?"

While Francis was preparing a convent for her, Sister Clare remained in the Benedictine house nearby and began her missionary work. In a short time, she had persuaded her sister Agnes to join her. There were now two members in her order. Gradually, the number increased and soon the first band of the Franciscan Order of Poor Ladies established themselves at St. Damien's — their first convent, adjoining the renowned chapel that Francis had repaired with his own hands. And thus began the Order of the Poor Clares founded by the lovely Clara Scifi in the year 1212.

When St. Clare was sick, she spent her time in making corporals for all the churches in and about Assisi. At length when she felt that she was to die she called all her sisters around her and told them they should never forget all the graces God had given them since they had become a religious family. The Pope himself came to visit her in her last illness. St. Agnes made the journey from her convent in Florence to be with her at the end. There were also three of the companions of St. Francis with her at the same time, Leo, Angelo and Juniper. Leo, who was a priest, read the Passion of Our Lord according to St. John, just as he had done for St. Francis twenty-seven years before, in 1226.

Her funeral took place from the Church of St. Damien, the Church which St. Francis had repaired with his own hands. Pope Innocent IV celebrated the Mass. Her body was carried to St. Damien's in a procession that resembled a grand triumph rather than a funeral.

St. Clare is still known is Assisi as "the chief rival of the Blessed Francis in the observance of Gospel perfection." She was declared a saint two years after her death and a great church was built in her honor.

> *The portals of Heaven opened*
> *For the coming of Sister Clare*
> *The Saint to be crowned in glory*
> *For her loving and tender care.*

PREACHING TO BIRDS

Francis once saw a great flock of birds in a field by the roadside. Drawing near to them he said, "Praise the Lord, my little sisters." Then they listened attentively while he told them how grateful they should be for their food, their sweet voices, their wings to fly with, their lovely feathers, and all the other good things which God had given them. At the end of the sermon he blessed them and they flew away singing joyfully.

STORY VI

How St. Francis Preached to Birds

St. Francis preached in gentle words
To God's small creatures — little birds!

St. Francis loved God very dearly. To prove this to Him, he considered two things — first, should he spend his whole life praying or should he go about the world preaching? He knew that prayer was very necessary if he wanted to save souls; but he also realized that he should try to spread devotion and love for Almighty God. So, after many days of pondering and wondering, Francis said, "I want my life to be as nearly like that of Christ as possible — I want to go to the poorest and the smallest of creatures and bring happiness to them, just as He brings joy and gladness to me."

His decision was made. Now, in the monastery with Francis lived his favorite friend, Brother Masseo. It was to him that Francis confided these words: "Go to the nearby convent, delivering this message to the saintly Sister Clare; tell her to pray fervently that God may show me what is best to do. Then proceed to the monastery to my faithful companion, Brother Silvester, asking him to pray also that I may be enlightened and strengthened to do God's Holy Will."

There was not a happier person in the countryside than Brother Silvester when he heard Francis' message from Brother Masseo. Happily and willingly, he consented to help, because, Brother Masseo said, "Did I not see a cross of gold coming from the mouth of Francis, which went lengthwise as far as Heaven, and the arms of which extended to the farthest corners of the earth?"

After a few moments of prayer, the saintly Silvester returned to Brother Masseo, saying, "God has counseled me to tell Brother Francis He has not chosen him for Himself, but that he might gain reward in the souls of others, and through him many might be saved."

Sister Clare's words were the same. You can imagine that Francis must have been overjoyed when he heard it was God's desire that he should go about the world preaching. He knew he would now have opportunity to be more like Our Lord. His only exclamation was, "God's will be done!" With this beautiful prayer on his lips, he started on his mission.

He decided it would be best to go through his native town, Assisi, and so his journey began. Traveling along the narrow stony road, he looked at the heavens spangled with stars.

And as he gazed at the beautiful blue sky, his thoughts traveled back to the time when he was a young boy and he recalled what his mother had once said to him, "You know, my dear, the stars are some of the most beautiful things that God has created. They are the islands of the blessed; they are the stopping places for the souls that are on their way to God; if you are good and honest and brave, some day you will have a home in one of them while you are waiting to be received into Heaven."

And now, he grew sad. Tonight there were only a few stars. There must have been a very small number of souls waiting for God! How he hoped that some night he might see the countless stars and say, "In the islands there are many who are blessed, because I have helped them."

He had now reached the little town of Savurniano. What a beautiful setting in which to speak about God! Peace and quiet were everywhere! God's wonderful works of creation gleamed all around him! The sky was as blue as Mary's mantle, the stars like glittering gold, the trees sheltered the birds and beasts, the earth in its silence, was waiting for words from Heaven!

When morning came he heard the swallows in the branches blithely singing. To them he spoke calling them his "little sisters." Why should he not preach them a sermon! As soon as he began, the singing ceased, and the birds listened with rapt attention. As the missioner of God concluded his words, townsfolk who had gathered, returned to their homes comforted and happy.

Still marveling at the beautiful surroundings, he continued his journey through other towns called Cannaio and Bevagno. As he looked at a particular tree, he noticed hundreds of tiny birds on the limbs, and his first thought was, "I must stop. I must preach also to these little sisters."

"Be grateful, O birds," he said, "for you owe much to God, your Creator. You should always praise Him, for He has given you liberty to fly to all places; He has given you feathers to cover you; you have fountains and brooks where you can quench your thirst; you have mountains and valleys for refuge. God loves you so much, He gives you trees in which to build your nests; beware then of ingratitude for it is a sin!"

And then came the great miracle! As Francis uttered his last words, the birds opened their beaks, stretched their necks, spread their wings, and reverently bowed their heads to the ground to prove by their acts of adoration that they revered God. They remained in this position until Francis made the Sign of the Cross over them. Then, to his great joy, the multitude of birds caroled sweetly and flew away.

The sermon had ended and Francis was ready to continue on his journey; however, he was not alone, for the hundreds and hundreds of swallows separated in the shape of a cross and going north, south, east and west, they resembled the golden cross that had come from the mouth of Francis – they too, would journey far to show their zeal in spreading God's holy gospel.

Francis' happiness knew no bounds. With a light heart and a burning desire to continue preaching, he set out for the next town. His gaze fell upon a field where grain had been harvested. Some birds were feeding on the wheat grains that had been left by the reapers. Francis was deeply moved by their beauty and forgot they were birds; he thought of them as his little brothers and sisters, who recognized at once his love for them. Fondly he stroked their necks and backs; tenderly, he wrapped some in his cloak; gently he said to all "Love God and praise God and thank God for all the wonderful things He has given you." They bowed to the ground and then, joining in song, scattered themselves and flew away. Francis said, "Thank God, my work for Him is not in vain."

The Saint's task was not easy. In fact, he worked so hard for many years that finally he became very tired. One September morning, he decided to go to a mountain top where he could rest. He climbed wearily over many rocks, until he reached a great oak tree. "How beautiful," he thought, "I think I shall lie here to rest." Suddenly the peaceful silence of the mountain was broken by music, by choruses and carols of unbounded joy. And then the sky grew very dark; Francis became a little disturbed, but in a flash he realized that the darkness was caused by thousands of birds which were spreading their wings in flight towards him. They had come to welcome their brother, their messenger from God. They perched on his head, shoulders, feet, and even filled the hood of his cloak.

"Dearest ones," he said, "it is very pleasant dwelling here, since all my friends are glad of my coming."

The Saint found great pleasure in the different sermons that he preached. He reproved himself to his friends because he had not thought to preach to them long before.

Monsignor Robert Hugh Benson tells us about these birds in such a way that one may easily remember all that happened. This is his poem:

"Once St. Francis of Assisi saw a crowd of little birds
So he preached a sermon to them, and they listened to his
words;

" 'Praise the Lord, my little Sisters, for the Lord, your God
is good;

In the ark that Noah made He saved your fathers from the
flood.'

"Pleased because he called them 'sisters,' all the birds spread
out their wings

And flew down to Brother Francis, who could say such
pretty things.

" 'Praise the Lord, my little sisters, for the Lord, your God
is good,

And He gives you trees for houses, streams for drink and
grain for food.'

"Then they stretched their necks and bowed their heads until
they touched the sod,

While he told them they must study always to give praise
to God.

"Lastly with the Cross he blessed them, and their faith the
birds confessed,

Flying off in four battalions, North and South and East and
West.

"Out of all the lovely deeds that Francis did at sweet Assisi,

I have chosen only this, because its lesson is so easy;

" 'Praise the Lord, and love His creatures, bird and beast, as
well as men.'

Sweet St. Francis of Assisi, would that he were here again."

TAMING THE WOLF

Returning to Italy he resumed his missionary life. At Gubbio he found the inhabitants terrified by a fierce wolf which not only killed their cattle but attacked and slew men. Francis went out alone and unarmed in search of the beast. When the wolf rushed at him the holy man made a sign of the cross, upon which the wolf lay down at his feet and became henceforth as meek as a lamb.

How Saint Francis Tamed the Wolf

"Through faith in God and His holy cross
St. Francis conquered — he suffered no loss."

A very familiar figure in the streets of Gubbio, a little old Italian city, was Francis. Most of the townspeople wondered what kind of a person he might be. Many considered him foolish because he mortified himself by penance and gave up all kinds of pleasure, to please God and atone for sins. More than once he was the victim of severe beatings and stonings as he walked through the narrow streets, but he ignored the cruel offenders, always exclaiming, "I suffer all for God."

Now, it happened that while Francis was living in Gubbio, a wolf appeared there, the most terrible and fierce of the country. It attacked not only animals, but also men and even children. Everyone was frightened because this dangerous animal came into the city, day and night, when least expected.

The people of Gubbio were afraid to walk the streets until one among them, the gentlest man of the whole city, was brave enough to try to conquer the animal. It was none other than poor Francis. His friends begged him not to go, saying "Stay, Francis, it is too dangerous an undertaking."

Laughingly and without hesitation, he answered, "Dangerous? Never! Not when God is with me!" So, making the Sign of the Cross, he left the place and set out on his mission.

Now, because Francis did not live very near the people of the village, he did not know very much about what was happening as he started forth. However, for many months the farmers' barnyards had been robbed every night of chickens, lambs and sheep. On many a night, the people of the village would be awakened by the poor victims of the hunger of the beast. They decided to put an end to the wolf's actions. They were determined to kill him, so there would be no more stealing, killing or attacking.

By the next morning, they had succeeded in capturing the beast and were ready to beat him to death, when — lo! a humble, quiet figure descended from the mountain. Francis raised his hand and the battle between the wolf and the men stopped. The messenger of peace had come to restore order to the little community.

Word spread like wildfire that the monk named Francis was about to tame the wolf. A great crowd gathered to witness a miracle.

Bravely, courageously, Francis approached the wolf who at once sprang at him with opened mouth. Everyone gasped for each thought that in a moment the monk would be be torn to pieces by the animal. Calmly and serenely, however, Francis raised his right hand, making the Sign of the Cross over the animal.

"Come along, Brother Wolf," he said, "you are guilty and I command you on the part of Christ to do no harm to me or to anyone else."

A deathlike silence fell upon the crowd. The very men who had despised Francis until this day, now looked upon him with awe and admiration. He was performing a miracle before their eyes, for as he spoke his commanding words, the terrible wolf closed his mouth and like a gentle lamb lay down to rest at the feet of Francis. By the power of God, Francis transformed the most terrible and ravaging of beasts into the mildest and tamest of pets.

"Brother Wolf," said Francis, "You have done much damage in this country; you've done many evil deeds, killing God's creatures without His permission; you have destroyed the cattle — that is bad enough — but, what is worse, you have killed creatures made to the image and likeness of God; a murderer and a thief, you deserve to be hanged. But, Brother Wolf, remember the greatest of all was put to death by such as you are, and He, in His endless goodness and kindness, for-

FOUNDING OF THE THIRD ORDER

At this time Francis founded the Third Order of Penance for those who wished to lead a life of perfection but who could not, for one reason or another, leave the world. The first to be received into this Third Order were Luchesio and Bonadonna, holy married people living in the city of Poggibonsi.

gave. So I, too, His servant will forgive you. I will make peace between your and the villagers, and there will be no more persecution."

And miracle — at the sound of these words, the wolf penitently moved his body, his tail and his eyes, telling Francis that he was ready to obey.

"I think," said Francis, "that it was hunger that caused you to do so much evil, so if I arrange to have food given to you daily, will you promise never again to harm man or beast?"

As a sign of recognition and agreement, Brother Wolf gently bowed his head. The crowd, amazed and overcome, repented that they had ever hated Francis; they wished that they might be like him. They realized that Francis had this great power because he was good — they knew he loved God and lived for Him alone. These thoughts ran through their minds as they heard Francis ask the wolf to promise never to do harm again — "It is not enough for you to bow your head; I want a pledge." Then in a flash, the animal lifted his right paw, gently placing it in Francis' hand, pledging "Peace forevermore!"

The amazed spectators spread the news of this miracle throughout the village. In a very short time, Francis was surrounded by a great throng of eager villagers.

Francis spoke to the multitude, impressing upon them

the need of penance and grace to combat trouble and sin. His beautiful sermon ended thus: "Remember, brothers, much more terrible are the flames of hell than the fangs of the wolf." The fangs of the wolf can destroy only the body but the deadly fangs of sin will destroy the soul. He made them realize that if they were afraid of a little dumb animal, how much more frightened they should be of the terrible animal called sin.

Noticing a shudder pass through his audience, Francis advised: "Since you realize the danger and because you have seen and heard the pledge of Brother Wolf, do likewise and promise to help him to keep his treaty of peace." As the crowd promised to fulfill this pledge, the wolf gently swayed his body, tail and ears and again raising his right paw, placed it in the hand of his master.

The "despised hermit" had become a "prince of men." By the power of God he had saved his countrymen, friends and enemies alike, from a cruel and ferocious beast. Through his love for God, he had put himself in danger of being instantly devoured by the beast that he had transformed into a mild and genle lamb.

For two years, the wolf lived peacefully in Gubbio, going from door to door, doing harm to no one. He followed Francis through the streets of Gubbio, just as a little dog might follow one down the street to school.

Page Eighty-eight

This was but one of the many miracles God allowed a favorite saint to perform! Remember, at the same time, that He loves us just as much; but, of course, He expects us to return that love just as Francis did. He expects us to obey just as the people obeyed Francis when they fed the wolf for two years after its conversion. One day it wandered into the market place, lay down very quietly and died. The villagers who had come to love the "good wolf" carried him to the spot where he had been transformed as into a lamb, and buried him. A small, crude headstone was erected over its grave bearing the inscription "Here lies the good wolf of Gubbio – little brother of St. Francis."

The wolf was conquered by a man
Who lived for God above,
He banished fear from every place
And brought in peace and love.

REBUILDING ST. DAMIEN'S

Francis did not forget what the Crucifix of San Damiano had told him to do. Having returned to Assisi, he secured a number of stones which he laboriously carried down to San Damiano himself. There he set to work to repair the old church, aided by some good-natured passers-by.

STORY VIII

Brother Juniper

Juniper, faithful and pious and true,
Helped to rebuild God's temple anew!

In the beginning when Francis had set out to fulfill God's command to rebuild the church of St. Damien, there was among the twelve who came to be Francis' helpers in his great work one named Juniper. Because of his kindness and charity, Francis loved Juniper very dearly. Many times he had watched him giving food and clothing to beggars. Often he had seen this "brother" playing with the children in the street.

"Ah," thought Francis, "Brother Juniper must hold a very high place in the Court of Heaven, for Christ Himself has said 'Unless you become as little children, you shall not enter the kingdom of Heaven!' "

When less childlike brethren teased Juniper and made fun of him, he always remained silent and in his heart prayed that his child-like actions would please Almighty God. He felt sad and troubled when others mocked him, saying that

he was doing nothing, that he was spending his time foolish-
ly, that he was not laboring for the glory of God.

But, then, his saddened heart became glad again as he
remarked, "God became the Saviour of mankind by becom-
ing a little child; He begged 'little children to come unto
Him' — He promised Heaven to those 'who would be as little
children —' Why should I not try to live in the manner that
God likes best?"

Francis loved Juniper for his sincerity and humility.
When Brother Juniper felt that his fine robe and cord were
too good for him, he refused to wear them.

When Juniper gave away his possessions to the poor,
Francis exclaimed: "Would that we had a whole forest of
Junipers!"

As Christmas approached, Francis and his disciples
made elaborate preparations for the feast. They did their
best to make the altar more beautiful than ever. Having obtained a fringe of gold adorned with large silver bells, the
sacristan entrusted to Juniper the task of guarding the
altar.

Almost as soon as Juniper had taken his post he saw a
poor woman begging alms in the name of Christ. For a moment Juniper was silent; then suddenly he said, "Ah, yes;
nothing is too good for God's poor. God doesn't need those
silver bells on the altar — I'll give those to you."

Page Ninety-four

Dumbfounded, the woman looked on as Juniper took out his knife and cut the bells from the fringe. He gave them to her, wishing her God-speed on her way.

The sacristan returned to complete the last few details in the decoration of the altar. His dismay was great when he realized that the silver bells were no longer there.

"I should have known better than to leave that Juniper around anything that might be given to the poor. Without doubt he has given the bells to some beggar."

Enraged, the sacristan looked for Juniper, who calmly answered his rebukes by saying, "Oh, brother; do not be angry with me for that poor woman needed them more than God."

Refusing to listen to the words which he considered foolish, the sacristan started out to search for the woman who had obtained the bells. But no luck! In vain, he went from one end of the city to the other! Yet, the object of his search never came into his sight.

Downhearted and discouraged, he returned to the monastery, with the thought that the decorations on the altar would not be complete for the great feast of Christmas.

That evening, Brother Juniper was called before the Father Superior to be corrected for his fault. As the Father Superior raised his voice scolding Juniper he became quite hoarse and Juniper began to wonder how he might find a remedy for him. After the Superior had dismissed him for the night he went into the city for a dish of porridge and butter. The distance was great, when he returned the preparation of the porridge required some time, so it was near midnight when he finally came to the cell of the Superior with a candle in one hand and the dish in the other. "What is this?" he was asked. "My father, when you reproved me today for my faults, I noticed that your voice became hoarse — I think that it must have been through excess of fatigue; and therefore I considered how to find a remedy, and had this porridge made for you; therefore I pray you eat it, for I assure you it will soften your chest and your throat." The good Father replied: "What an hour is this to come and disturb people!" And Brother Juniper said: "See, it is made on purpose for you; I pray you eat it, for it will do you a great deal of good." The answer came that he had no desire to eat and told Juniper to go away. "Then," said Juniper, "since you will not eat, and this porridge was made on purpose for you, do this much for me, hold the candle, and I will eat it." Then the Superior looking at Juniper as he sat on the floor of the cell relented and joined him in the repast and together they consumed the porridge.

The report of this incident greatly pleased Francis, because he thought that now the brother companions were recognizing the worth of poor Juniper, whom they had formerly scorned; he said, "They would all be good Friars if they could conquer the world and themselves like Brother Juniper."

Once Juniper went away to stay in a very small house belonging to the brothers. On a certain day, it happened that all the brothers were obliged to go out, and Juniper alone remained to prepare the meals and have refreshments ready when the friars returned.

"Leave it to me," he answered, as he received his assignment from the Guardian. Then he began to think – "How foolish that one person should spend so much time in the kitchen, losing precious moments for prayer. I know how I can fix that; I'll cook enough now for a whole fortnight!"

So he started off to the market place taking with him several large pots. These he filled with chickens, eggs and herbs. After returning, he placed chickens, feathers and all, and the other food in earthenware pots over a raging fire.

As the crazily cooked amount of food was placed on the table, Juniper was not praised for his great idea. So the poor friar fell to the floor to do penance for his misdeed; however, he could not understand why the brothers refused to eat the meal, because he had prepared it with good intentions.

Juniper was so humble that he was always ready to consider himself in the wrong. He was ever prompt to repent. To such an extent was he sincere that everyone admired him and his charity won for him the love of all who knew him.

> *The poor man of Assisi*
> *Had found a faithful friend*
> *In Juniper so simple*
> *And true unto the end.*

RECEIVING COMMUNION FROM BROTHER LEO

Francis had retired to his beloved Mount Alvernia where he felt himself farther from men and nearer to God. There he spent his days in prayer and fasting, in the company of the faithful Brother Leo, who who said Mass for him in a small cave on the rocky mountainside.

STORY IX

Brother Leo

To Brother Leo, Francis talked
Of perfect joy as on they walked.

Among the followers of St. Francis was one very dear to him who was called Brother Leo. He was born and brought up in Assisi and was among the first to join him. He was the Saint's constant companion and travelled with him on his journeys. He was the one who celebrated the Holy Mass in Greccio on the Christmas when the Crib was first made. When St. Francis was near death he wrote a blessing for Brother Leo, and a letter, both of which may be seen in Assisi. St. Francis called him "his little brother sheep of God."

As these two were once going along the road on their way to the church of St. Mary of the Angels, the Saint showed to Leo "the things which were perfect joy." It was the winter time and both were suffering from the cold when St. Francis said: "O Brother Leo, though the friars give a good example of sanctity, write it down and note it well that this is not perfect joy." When they had gone on a little further he added: "O Brother Leo, even though the friars should give sight to the blind, hearing to the deaf, speech to the dumb, power of walking to the lame and should raise to life those who had been dead four days, write this down, that in all this there is not perfect joy."

Then for a third time he cried out a little more loudly: "O Brother Leo, if the friars knew all languages, and all the sciences and all the scriptures, and if they could prophesy, and tell the future and the secrets of consciences and souls, write this down that in all this there is not perfect joy." After a few more steps he shouted again: "O Brother Leo, thou little sheep of God, though the friars spoke with the tongues of angels and knew the course of the stars and the virtues of herbs and though to them were revealed the treasures of the earth and the virtues of birds and fishes, of all animals and men, of trees and stones and roots and waters, write it down that this is not perfect joy." Advancing further along the way he called out: "O Brother Leo, though the friars should convert all infidels to the faith of Christ by their preaching, write also that this is not perfect joy."

Two miles of the journey had been passed while these questions and answers were being proposed when Brother Leo asked, "In the name of God, tell me then what is perfect joy." St. Francis replied in this way. "When we come to St. Mary of the Angels, soaked with rain, frozen with cold, covered with mud, and weak with hunger, and knock at the door, should someone come and ask in anger, 'Who are you?' and we should reply, 'Two of your brethren' and he should say: 'You are not telling the truth; you are two good-for-nothings who go about stealing from the poor, now go away.' And if he would not open the door to us, but kept us outside in the night and the rain, in the cold and wind, in hunger and thirst, and if we would bear this abuse and cruelty patiently without murmuring, and should think humbly and charitably of him and think that he knew us truly and that he spoke as God would have him speak against us, write that this would be perfect joy.

"Suppose then we should continue to knock after he had closed the door against us and he should come out and drive us away by force, saying: 'Leave this house, you pair of thieves; go to the poor-house, you can get nothing to eat and no place to stay in this house.' If we should bear this with patience, with joy and love, write O Brother Leo, that this would be perfect joy.

"And then if the hunger, the cold and the night made us bold enough to return and beg of him through the door for the love of God to let us in, and then hear his voice condemning us as rascals and beggars and telling us he will give us what we deserve as he came out in fury with a big stick to beat us and throw us down and roll us in the snow or mud; should we bear these things with patience and joy thinking of the pains of the Blessed Lord as what we should bear for His love, write O Brother Leo, that this would be perfect joy.

"Now, here is the conclusion Brother Leo: better than all the graces and gifts of the Holy Spirit which Christ has given to His friends is that of conquering oneself and suffering for the love of Him all pain and insult and calamity. Here is the reason: in all other gifts of God we cannot glory, seeing they are not ours but His, for the Apostle has said: 'What hast thou that thou hast not received? And if thou hast received it, why glory in it as if thou hadst it of thyself?' But we may glory in the cross of tribulation and affliction for these are ours, and therefore says St. Paul, 'I will not glory save in the cross of Our Lord Jesus Christ.'"

Brother Leo lived for almost fifty years after St. Francis. He saw the followers of the Saint increase to such an extent that Franciscans were to be seen everywhere. Many of them became missionaries and martyrs for the faith in far away lands. The Third Order for people in the world became established in all the countries of Europe. Popes, Kings and Queens belonged to it and tried their best to live according to the Rule written for them by St. Francis. Brother Leo had a great part in directing the progress of the Order and brought it success because he was faithful to everything he had learned from its Founder. The holy Rule taken from the Gospel was preserved by him and followed in all its fulness by those whom he persuaded to become Franciscans.

Because Leo had been with Francis every day from the time he joined the Saint as one of his early companions, he knew him and his ideas better than any one else. Just as the Apostles knew our Lord better than others as they were with Him and heard Him speak and teach, so did this holy priest know the little poor man of Assisi and wrote down what he had seen and heard while in his company. Whatever has been written about St. Francis and his times, what he did for the Church, how he converted souls and made them love God, peace and charity, can be traced back to the writings of this faithful companion. He watched over the brethren and also over the order of Saint Clare, helped her to found convents for her nuns and was with her when she died. Remembering how St. Francis had gone to God and the prayers he recited at the time, he did the same for her who was to be honored by the side of the great Saint Francis of Assisi.

> *His hope in life was not for gold*
> *Nor was his search for fame*
> *But joy eternal which he found*
> *In the Saviour's Holy Name.*

THE STIGMATA

On the feast of Holy Cross before day-break the man of God was praying on the mountain. Suddenly he saw flying down from heaven towards him, the figure of a Seraph, bearing the likeness of Christ on the Cross. The soul of Francis was fired with divine love, and when the vision disappeared he saw that his hands, feet and side bore the five wounds of Our Lord's Passion.

Death of Saint Francis

The vision of Christ on the mountain so high
Revealed to St. Francis that Death's call was nigh.

Francis had labored for many years in his vocation to make everyone love God. He had done everything possible to be like Christ. No task was too great for him, no burden was too heavy. Having spent the greater part of his life in tireless efforts to do all he could, he realized that he had not so much strength as formerly. He had become very weak and was almost blind. A painful operation had been performed on his eyes which did not cure them. In the year 1224, when he was about forty-three years of age, he received from a certain Orlando, who had a great veneration for him, a mountain in Tuscany, called Alvernia. There he decided to spend some time in penance and prayer. To the brethren he said: "My sons, we are approaching a lenten fast of St. Michael the Archangel; I am persuaded that it is the will of God we should pass this Lent on the Mount Alvernia, on which by Divine Providence a place has been prepared for us that, to the honor and glory of God and His glorious Virgin

Mother Mary and of the holy angels, we may, through penance, merit to receive from Christ the consolation of consecrating this blessed mountain."

In his little hut on the mountain top, Francis prayed that "his brothers" would not forget to take care of his poor. Many times he prayed all night long. On one of these occasions, the seventeenth of September, there appeared to him "a seraph having six wings, bearing a beautiful man whose hands and feet were outstretched on a cross." As the vision approached, Francis marveled at the beauty of the seraph, yet his heart was sad at the sight of the Cross. It remained only a short time, but while fading out of sight, it left upon his hands and feet the impression of nails – like those of the Cross. On his right side was the mark of a wound from which bright red blood flowed, staining his robe.

He could hardly believe what he saw – he thought himself unworthy to be chosen by Christ in this manner. The glory of such an honor overwhelmed him. After having spent forty days on the mountain top, he decided to return to Assisi.

There he found St. Clare, the one who had helped him most, the one whom he admired more than any other. With her he spent happy moments, realizing that, more than all others, she was true to her ideals in loving and caring for the sick and poor. "They are now my own particular friends," were her parting words to Francis. Could any words have made him happier?

Now Francis realized that God had given him unusual graces because of the many miracles which he had performed in healing the sick; so he asked Him the favor of restoring his health, always adding, "If it be Your Holy Will." Hopefully, he awaited the opinion of his physician, who told him that his condition was serious and that he was near death.

These were the words for which Francis had secretly awaited. Praising God, he begged his companions to carry him to the Portiuncula — to die there in peace with God alone.

The Portiuncula was the spot St. Francis loved best on earth, and it was his dying gift to his companions. He begged them never to leave it, saying: "If you are driven out by one door, come in again by the other, for this place is holy and is the House of God. When there were only a few of us here, God brought others to join us; here He enlightened our minds with His wisdom and enflamed our hearts with His love. Here, if you pray with devotion, you will obtain what you ask, but if you offend God here, you will be more severely punished. Therefore, children, honor this place and sing therein forever the praises of God."

As he was being carried by his brothers to the Chapel, he asked to be placed on the ground, his face towards the city that he might invoke a blessing upon Assisi. He called it a holy city because it had been faithful to God and because through the Franciscan Order of which it was the birthplace, many souls would be saved. When he had finished speaking, the little procession went on to St. Mary of the Angels where he was placed in the hut which served as an infirmary.

Some days before his death, Francis had thought of the Lady Jacobi di Settessoli who had been a generous benefactor to him in Rome. "Brother Jacomina", as he called her used to make little cakes, called marzipan, of almonds and sugar which he liked very much. He now wished one of his brothers to write asking her to bring gray cloth for his shroud and some of the little cakes. When the letter was written, Francis told the brother it would not be necessary to send it to Rome. A few minutes later the Lady Jacobi and her two sons were at the door with the very things the Saint had desired her to bring. She remained with him until his death.

The night before he died, in imitation of Christ, he begged the brothers to bring bread to him. Blessing and breaking it, he distributed it to "his disciples" saying, "I have done my part —" "may Christ teach you to do yours."

As St. Francis had always loved the birds and had preached to them in the fields, so now God sent them to sing farewell before his death. The larks were his favorites, and at sunset of his last day on earth, a great number of them came and sang softly outside the window of the room where he lay.

The next evening, October 3rd, in the year 1226, Francis died singing the words of the one hundred and forty-first psalm:

"I cried to thee, O Lord: I said: Thou art my hope, my portion in the land of the living.

"Attend to my supplication: for I am brought very low.

"Bring my soul out of prison, that I may praise thy name: the just wait for me, until thou reward me."

Perhaps Francis' outstanding title to a heavenly crown of glory was his boundless love for God's poor. Clothing, feeding, sheltering them, the kind and holy Friar always kept in mind these words: "Amen, I say to you, as long as you did it, to one of these, my least brethren, you did it to me."

The poorest and lowest of creatures were closest to the heart of Francis, because they were God's chosen ones. Francis modeled his life so closely to that of Christ that

"When his Maker from the thrall of earth
His spirit freed,
No suffering accompanied the call.
Mercy then decreed,
One moment here, the next
To be in Heaven for all eternity."

BLESSING ASSISI

Saint Francis was grievously ill and nearing his end. He asked the Brothers to carry him down from Assisi to Saint Mary of the Angels where he wished to die. On the way there they stopped and turned round so that he should face towards his native town. He gave the city his last blessing and thanked God for all the good He had bestowed on it and on its inhabitants.

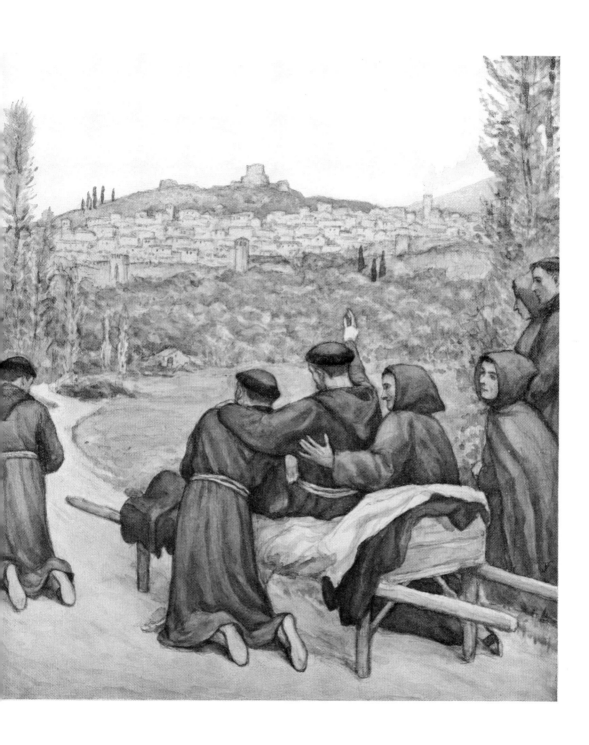

AFTERWORD

On October 4th, the body of St. Francis was borne by his "brothers" through Assisi. The city was adorned with flowers and hangings, and great crowds of people thronged the streets through which the solemn procession passed. A few days before his death, the Saint had promised to visit Clare and her daughters. Now to fulfill his promise, his body was carried to St. Damien's. Through the grill of the chapel the Sisters venerated the sacred stigmata and bade a last farewell to their Father.

Francis had wished to be buried on the *Colle d'Inferno,* "the condemned hill," because it was the burying place of criminals. Francis thought – "They are the poorest and most despised of creatures, but they still belong to God – and I choose to be buried with them." He was sure that no one would honor him after death, if he was buried in such a place, but the people came in crowds to his tomb begging his help in all their misfortunes. So many miracles were performed there, that on July 16, 1228, the Pope himself went to Assisi and with great pomp and ceremony, declared Francis a Saint. Two years later his remains were transferred and placed under the high altar of the great church erected in his honor.

VENERATION OF SAINT CLARE

The funeral procession on its way to Assisi, stopped at San Damiano, in order that Saint Clare and her sisters might see their father for the last time. They kissed the wounds on his hands and wept piteously at their grave loss. Then, amid a crowd of people carrying torches and olive branches, the relics of the saint made their triumphal entry into the city.

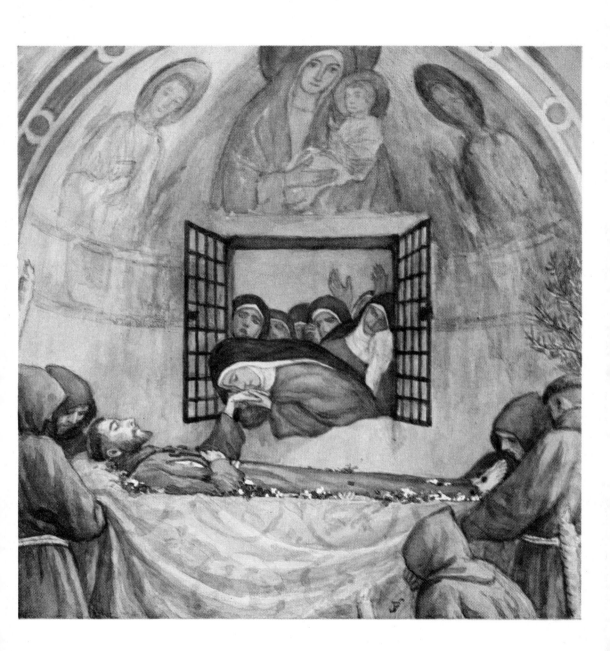

How St. Francis Spoke and Wrote

HIS VOCATION

"In His mercy, God has called us, not alone for our personal sanctification, but for the salvation of a great number. We must go through the world, preaching more by example, than by word; and arousing all men to do penance for their sins and to keep the commandments of God... Fear nothing...and be strongly resolved in your hearts to endure everything with patience and humility."

HIS BLESSING

And whosoever shall observe God's will let him be filled in heaven with the blessing of His beloved Son, together with the Most Holy Spirit, the Paraclete, and all the powers of heaven, and all the Saints. And I, Brother Francis, your servant, in so far as I can, confirm unto you within and without this most holy blessing.

HIS EXHORTATION

O Beloved Brethren and Children, eternally blessed, listen to me, listen to the voice of your Father. We have promised great things, but greater are promised to us. Let us observe the former and sigh after the latter. Pleasures are short, the punishment is eternal. Sufferings are light, the glory is infinite. Many are called, few are chosen; there will be retribution for all.

HIS PRAYER FOR PEACE

Lord, make me an instrument of your peace. Where there is hatred, let me sow love; where there is injury, pardon; where there is doubt, faith; where there is despair, hope; where there is darkness, light; and where there is sadness, joy. O, divine Master, grant that I may not so much seek to be consoled as to console; be understood as to understand; be loved as to love; for it is in giving that we receive; it is in pardoning that we are pardoned; and it is in dying that we are born to eternal life.

HIS RULE

"Blessed Francis, seeing that the Lord God was daily increasing the number of the brethren, for that very purpose wrote down simply and in a few words for himself and for his brethren, both present and future, a pattern and rule of life, using chiefly the language of the holy Gospel after whose perfection alone he yearned."

Thomas of Celano

St. Francis said of it: This rule will be for the brethren the book of life, the hope of salvation, the marrow of the Gospel, the way of perfection, the key of Paradise and the Covenant of an eternal alliance.

Page One Hundred and Twenty-four

HIS ADVICE

Consider the vocation to which God has called you, not only for your own salvation, but for that of many, that we may go through the world exhorting men more by our example than by our words to do penance for their sins, and to remember the Commandments of God. Do not fear, though you be weak and ignorant, but announce penance simply, confiding in God Who has conquered the world, for His Spirit will speak in you and will exhort all men to be converted and to keep God's commandments. You will find some men faithful, meek and kind, who will receive you with joy and who will keep and hear your words. You will find others — and these more numerous — who are unfaithful and proud; they will resist you and what you will say to them. Take therefore, the resolution to support everything with patience and humility. Then after some time many men will come to you, some of them noble and learned and will go with you to preach to the kings, the princes, and the people. And many will return to God, Who will increase and multiply His family in the entire world.

HIS BLESSING OF ASSISI

Blessed be thou of God, O holy city, because by thee shall many souls be saved, and in thee many servants of God shall dwell, and from out of thee shall many be elected to the kingdom of eternal life.

A Canticle of St. Francis

Among the genuine writings of St. Francis, is this Canticle. It was composed in the form of a hymn, in 1225, in the garden of the Church of St. Damien. Just before his death in the following year, he added the verses to his "Sister Death." The Praises of Creatures is another name by which it is known. The Saint's love of nature as the creation of God is given an expression as reasonable as it is poetical. He found in all that God has made a reflection of the Goodness, the Wisdom and the Beauty of the Creator.

O most mighty, omnipotent, and good Lord,

To Thee belong praise, honor, and all benediction!

To Thee alone, Most High, are all these due.

There is no man worthy Thy name to speak.

Praise be to Thee, my Lord, with all Thy creatures!

And above all for our brother, the Sun,

Who gives us light in the day;

And he is beautiful and radiant with great splendor.

Of Thee, Most High, he is the sign.

Praise be to Thee for Sister Moon and the Stars,

Which Thou madest for heaven, clear, rare and beautiful!

Praise to Thee, my Lord, for Brother Wind,

For air and clouds, for quiet time and stormy,

A Canticle of Saint Francis

By which Thou dost sustain all Thy creatures!

Praise to Thee, my Lord, for Sister Water,

Useful and humble, and precious and chaste!

Praise to Thee, my Lord, for Brother Fire,

Who lightens up the night,

And is handsome and joyous and robust and able!

Praise to Thee, my Lord, for our sister and mother,

The Earth, who brings forth varied fruit and herbs, bright-
hued,

Who sustains and keeps us.

Praise to Thee for those who forgive for love of Thee

Sustaining afflictions and tribulations!

Blessed be those who keep themselves in peace!

By Thee, Most High, will they be crowned at last.

Praise to Thee, my Lord, for Sister Death,

From whom no man can flee!

But woe to those who die in mortal sin!

Blessed are those who do Thy most holy will!

To them the second death can bring no evil.

Praise ye, and bless my Lord, and thank Him, and serve Him
with great humility!

HIS BLESSING FROM THE BIBLE

The Lord bless thee, and keep thee.

The Lord shew his face to thee, and have mercy on thee.

The Lord turn his countenance to thee, and give thee peace.

Numbers VI; 24, 25, 26